The Dream of Gerontius

THE DREAM OF GERONTIUS

I went to sleep.

THE DREAM OF
GERONTIUS

BY JOHN HENRY CARDINAL NEWMAN
ILLUSTRATED BY : :
STELLA LANGDALE
WITH AN INTRODUCTION
BY GORDON TIDY

LONDON : JOHN LANE THE BODLEY HEAD
NEW YORK : JOHN LANE COMPANY MCMXVI

WILLIAM BRENDON AND SON, LTD., PRINTERS, PLYMOUTH, ENGLAND

LIST OF ILLUSTRATIONS

"There are, on the other hand, thousands for whom Newman's writings belong, to use Dean Stanley's phrase—'not to provincial dogma, but to the literature of all time.' He is for them the author of the Oxford Sermons, with their matchless insight into human nature; the religious poet who wrote *The Dream of Gerontius* and *Lead, kindly Light*; while *The Apologia* belongs in their eyes to the literature of self-revelation, not to apologetic."

WILFRID WARD, *The Life of John Henry Cardinal Newman*

"In 1866 Newman's last and greatest poem appeared. In *The Dream of Gerontius* it would seem as though there had been gathered up all the forces that had for so many years been restrained, and the poet, when he is already approaching his three score and ten years, shows us, in a sudden blaze of almost intolerable light, the high and awful thoughts that devout meditation and self-suppression have stored up in a mind compounded of reverence and imagination, for which poetic expression was the only natural outlet."

FREDERIC CHAPMAN, *Introduction to the Poems of John Henry Newman*

"*The Dream of Gerontius* was the true copestone for Newman to cut and to lay on the literary and religious work of his whole life. Had Dante himself composed *The Dream of Gerontius* as his elegy on the death of some beloved friend, it would have been universally received as altogether worthy of his superb genius, and it would have been a jewel altogether worthy of his peerless crown. There is nothing of its kind outside of the *Purgatorio* and the *Paradiso* at all equal to the *Gerontius* for solemnising, ennobling, and sanctifying power. It is a poem that every man should have by heart who has it before him to die."

ALEXANDER WHYTE, D.D., *Newman: An Appreciation in two Lectures*

INTRODUCTION

B

INTRODUCTION

LMOST all those who have written of Cardinal Newman as a poet have mentioned what may be termed the history of *The Dream of Gerontius*. And indeed it is a subject that has its proper place in the history of literature, and so evidently possesses an interest for every " letter'd heart."

This history of the poem has commonly begun with a legend which such writers as are referred to above have been at pains to perpetuate.

Thus Henry J. Jennings, in his *Cardinal Newman*, wrote : " The story runs that this sublime composition was so lightly valued by Dr. Newman that he had consigned, or was about to consign, it to the waste-paper basket, when a lucky accident led to its rescue, the quick appreciation of some discriminating critic, and its subsequent publication."

Similarly Richard Holt Hutton, in his contribution to the " English Leaders of Religion " series, has stated : " Newman had written a poem of which he himself thought so little, that it was, as I have heard, consigned

3

or doomed to the waste-paper basket ; and Mr. Jennings, in his very interesting account of Cardinal Newman, credits the statement. Some friend who had eyes for true poetry rescued it, and was the means therefore of preserving to the world one of the most unique and original of the poems of the present century."

And Dr. William Barry, in the *Newman* of the " Literary Lives " series, speaking of " a dramatic poem," stated that its author " was not satisfied with it, and flung the manuscript aside. By good hap one saw it that had eyes, rescued the pages from the dark, and persuaded him to let others read it. The poem thus perilously nigh to destruction proved to be *The Dream of Gerontius*." ·

The same writer, in the *Catholic Cyclopædia*, also says of the poem that it " had been nearly a lost masterpiece."

Again, William E. A. Axon, in an article which appeared in *The Library* (1905), and which was entitled " The Dream of Gerontius," began by saying : " *The Dream of Gerontius* is one of those famous books that has had a narrow escape from destruction. John Henry Newman's thoughts had long been turned to the grave, and on the death of a friend he put his musings into the form of a dramatic poem, but was not satisfied with the result, and cast the MS. aside. It was accidentally seen and rescued by one who succeeded in persuading the

4

author to publish the poem. Thus the world came into the possession of the *Dream of Gerontius.*"

(And Axon here appended a footnote which ran, " Newman, by William Barry.")

Thus may we see something of the way in which a story slips from pen to pen. Jennings hands it on to Hutton, and Barry to Axon, and from such sources it is not surprising that it has spread to other pages. A prefatory " Publisher's Note," for example, to a current presentation of the poem, contains the statement that " it is interesting to note that Cardinal Newman thought so lightly of the work that, but for the fortunate intervention of a friend with a true eye for poetry, it would have been consigned to the waste-paper basket."

It seems to have been Aubrey de Vere who, as far as the general public were concerned, first put an authoritative end to this fable. In the September number of the *Nineteenth Century* for 1896, in an article entitled " Some Recollections of Cardinal Newman " (which article was in the following year embodied with his *Recollections* volume) Aubrey de Vere wrote : " *The Dream of Gerontius*, as Newman informed me, owed its preservation to an accident. He had written it on a sudden impulse, put it aside, and forgotten it. The editor of a magazine wrote to him asking for a contribution. He looked into all his ' pigeon-holes,' and found nothing theological ; but in answering his correspondent he added that he had come upon some verses which, if, as editor, he cared to have, were at his command. The wise editor did care, and they were published at once."

There is no mention here of any dissatisfaction with the " verses," of any flinging of the manuscript aside, or of any discriminating friend, and the waste-paper basket is become a " pigeon-hole."

Another light-thrower upon this subject has been Edward Bellasis who, in his Introduction to the Presentation Edition—and Edward Bellasis spoke on such a subject with an authority which was final—definitely said, " The statement that it was put into the waste-paper basket is a legend."

If there should be any who should desire to write an essay on the Development of Literary Legend, such might find in the following extract matter for some useful illustration. It is taken from *Famous Hymns and their Authors*, by Francis Arthur Jones, and is to be found on p. 88 of the Third Edition of that work. Writing on Newman's famous hymn " Praise to the Holiest in the Height," Francis Arthur Jones found occasion to speak of the *Dream*, and he said : " Newman himself thought little of the poem at the time of writing it. Three years after its composition the editor of a religious magazine wrote to the cardinal asking him to contribute ' something ' to his paper. He was about to write and decline when he bethought himself of the

INTRODUCTION

Dream and sent it." In these three sentences there are certainly three positively false statements, nor is there any proof producible that, exactly in the sense intended by their writer, Newman himself thought little of the poem at the time of writing it. Indeed, as we shall see further on, there is ample reason why he should not, at the time of writing, have thought little of it.

Those who would wish to satisfy themselves or others as to what and where was the well-head of the Waste-paper Legend will be greatly helped to a theory by some words of Bellasis—of Bellasis who never wastes words.

Speaking, in his *Memorandum* on the MSS. of the *Dream of Gerontius*, of the "small bits of paper" on which the first rough draft of the poem was written, Bellasis said : " These were probably for the waste-paper basket."

And probably they were. But as that rough draft, or a part of it, has been reproduced in facsimile it is clear that the waste-paper basket was not, after all, its end. It is by no means unlikely that there actually was some chance and opportune visitor, and that that visitor did actually catch sight of those small bits of paper (as there were fifty-two of them they would be plain for all folk to see), and that seeing, or foreseeing, in them a relic of no small interest and importance, that visitor petitioned that their life might be spared. Nor is it difficult to believe that Newman would attach but little value to this rough draft—he had, we may well believe, waste-paper-basketed many and many an one during the previous forty-seven years of his literary life. And it seems easy to see how all this would get corrupted into a legend that Newman had doomed the poem to the waste-paper basket, whereas what he had really so doomed was that poem's first rough draft, whilst his small thought for that draft would be developed into such statements as the one that he "thought little of the poem at the time of writing it." Newman himself, be it observed, made no mention to Aubrey de Vere of his picturesque persuader to publish,—there was none to mention. But there very well may have been the reverent rescuer of a relic, someone who persuaded the poet not to destroy those fifty-two small bits of paper. Assuredly rough drafts, like books, have their destinies, and here was one, "probably" meant for the waste-paper basket, which, or a portion of which, nearly half a century after its reprieve, was to be reproduced in facsimile!

The Occasion What was the occasion of the writing of this poem? Jennings says: "The death-bed of a dear friend was the inspiring cause which occasioned *The Dream of Gerontius*." Barry writes: "On the death of a dear friend he had cast his musings into the form of a dramatic poem." Ernest Newman in his *Elgar* (John Lane) has written: "The poem was written by Cardinal Newman in 1865, under the stress of the

emotion caused him by the death of a dear friend."
M. Henri Bremond, in what is known to us in the H. C.
Corrance translation as *The Mystery of Newman,* speaks
of " the marvellous poem which the sexagenarian
Oratorian wrote on the recent grave of the dearest of
his brothers." But none of these, nor any of those who
have written in like manner, have given us the name of
the dear friend or of the dearest brother. Possibly it
has been the Dedication of the poem which has led such
writers so to write, although the " Most Beloved Brother,
John Joseph Gordon," of that Dedication died twelve
years before the poem was written. And there is perhaps
also a possibility that the date of the completion of the
poem almost exactly coinciding with the anniversary of
the Most Beloved Brother's death may have had something to do with such statements, as may have also the
fact that the year 1866 brought both the publication of
the *Dream* (in book-form) and the death of Keble.

Axon gives a most interesting account of how he was
himself informed by Professor Francis William Newman
that he had " suggested " to his brother " the subject of
the purification of a soul by penitential fires as a fitting
subject for a poem by one who believed in purgatory."

Axon, however, adds : " Cardinal Newman at a later
date, when asked if the poem had originated in his
brother's suggestion, declared that it had not." And
indeed the suggested subject would seem scarcely to be

the subject of the poem. But the truth is that the Cardinal had good grounds, when asked the question, for declaring " that it had not." For the true story of the occasion of the poem has been told us in Mr. Wilfrid Ward's *Life of John Henry, Cardinal Newman*, and a strange story it is.

It seems that " in the middle of the Kingsley controversy " Newman was " seized with a very vivid apprehension of immediately impending death, apparently derived from a medical opinion." This vivid apprehension caused him to write a " memorandum " headed " written in prospect of death," and which was, as Mr. Ward tells us, " dated Passion Sunday, 1864, 7 o'clock a.m." This " memorandum " Mr. Ward prints in full.

The " memorandum " may be called a Profession of Faith, and if it be not identical in word with the Profession of Faith given to Gerontius in the poem, it may be said to be identical with that Profession in all but word. And one observes the " I commit my soul. . . . Also to my tender Guardian Angel, and to all Angels, and to all Saints." Indeed it would appear impossible not to connect this " memorandum " written (as we have seen Mr. Ward writing) " with a very vivid apprehension of immediately impending death " with the poem's first verse—

Jesu, Maria—I am near to death.

INTRODUCTION

Moreover, the memorandum was written less than a year before the poem. One can but associate the memorandum's " because I do not know how long this perfect possession of my sensible and available health and strength may last," and its " written in prospect of death," with the lines—

> And through such waning span
> Of life and thought as still has to be trod,
> Prepare to meet thy God.

It was in the writing of this memorandum that the (as he very vividly apprehended) dying Newman did himself seek to

> Use well the interval.

And it should be noticed that the above quotations are the words of Gerontius.

So when Mr. Ward, alluding to the poem, tells us that Newman " set down in dramatic form the vision of a Christian's death on which his imagination had been dwelling," it is natural to conclude that that Christian's death had been his own.

And that it was his own would seem still further to be made probable by the choice of the name " Gerontius."

Axon has asked : " From whence did Newman take the name of Gerontius ? "

And Axon goes on to speak of a Roman general of

that name, and of how it was borne by " several persons " " mentioned in the ecclesiastical annals of the fourth and fifth centuries." And he ends his enquiry by saying: " It is a Latin adaptation of a Greek name, and suggests age." As Professor M. F. Egan, in his Introduction to the Annotated Edition of the poem, wrote: " Our young readers will please look up the derivation of Gerontius, which is from the Greek," and he gives a footnote which supplies the Greek word, the Greek word which means " an old man." This it is which connects the name of Gerontius with that of the poet. Writing from Rednall in April, 1865 (the year of the composition and publication of the poem), Newman said that he could not undertake certain literary engagements because " It is killing work to an old man." And in the previous year, in 1864, he had written to Sir Frederick Rogers: " But I am an old man," and in the same year he wrote to Dean Church making use of exactly the same expression, " but I am an old man." And to Father Ambrose St. John, and also in the year of the writing of the poem, he spoke of Keble, Pusey, and himself as " three old men."

The point appears to be worth consideration. For writers have speculated upon what manner of man Gerontius was or had been. Thus Alfred Austin, some time Poet Laureate, when writing on the poem (*The Poetry of the Period*) began his descriptive analysis with the words " A monk is dying." William Stebbing (*The Poets: Geoffrey Chaucer to Alfred Tennyson*) speaks of " the dying Saint's horror." Sir Francis Doyle (Oxford Lectures of 1868) said of Gerontius that he was " not apparently a man of any special or exceptional holiness." A. J. Jaeger, in his truly admirable analytical study of Elgar's *Dream*, has expressed his opinion that the composer regarded Gerontius " as an ordinary man and a sinner, who, after leading a worldly man's life is now ' near to death ' and repentant." All such opinions may have suggestive value for the student of the poem, though it is not quite easy to see what justification the poem provides for the theory that Gerontius had led " a worldly man's life." The truth is that it is hard to gather from the poem what manner of life had been that of Gerontius. But one thing that might be said would certainly seem to be that into his life a great love and appreciation of music had its decided place. It is the soul of Gerontius that exclaims :—

> And hark ! I hear a singing ; yet in sooth
> I cannot of that music rightly say
> Whether I hear or touch or taste the tones,
> Oh what a heart-subduing melody !

and

> But hark ! a grand mysterious harmony :
> It floods me, like the deep and solemn sound
> Of many waters.

and again—

> Hark ! for the lintels of the presence-gate
> Are vibrating and echoing back the strain.

And yet again (of the Demons)—

> How sour and how uncouth a dissonance !

Perhaps the threefold " There will I sing " of the exquisitely lovely last words of the Soul of Gerontius might be put into the same category. Bellasis in his *Cardinal Newman as a Musician* has applied the first of the above quotations to his subject's being " much affected by Beethoven." In all this there is, to say the least of it, a possible identification of the name of Gerontius with the name of Newman. Well and rightly did Barry speak of *The Dream of Gerontius* as " the grand Requiem which, like his beloved Mozart, the poet-philosopher composed against his journey home," and well and rightly also did he say in another place of how in the poem Newman " looked forward to his own pilgrimage, ' alone to the Alone.' "

With all this before us, and with before us that so significantly derived name of Gerontius, that reiterated " I am an old man," that " memorandum " which was written less than a year before the poem, it is perfectly permissible to connect the name of Gerontius most closely with Newman's own. And this, when now we proceed to the actual writing of the poem, will, by reason of that part of the writing of the poem which was its title, seem to be still further vindicated.

The Writing The *Dream* has often been described as "unique," and most assuredly the genesis of the poem was unique in the strictest sense of that epithet. What could read more surprisingly than the following sentences from a letter written by the poet to the Rev. John Telford, and printed by Wilfrid Ward: "You do me too much honour if you think I am to see in a dream everything that is to be seen in the subject dreamed about. I have said what I saw. . . . I have set down the dream as it came before the sleeper. It is not my fault if the sleeper did not dream more. Perhaps something woke him. Dreams are generally fragmentary." Here there is considerable stress laid upon the word "dream" and also on the word "sleeper." No one reading this letter for the first time but must perforce find a new meaning in the "Dream" of the title. Yet very important in these quoted words are the ones that tell of sight or vision: "If you think I am to *see* in a dream everything that is to be *seen*": "I have said what I *saw*." Bremond has told us that "Newman attached a serious importance to dreams." He might well attach a serious importance to the one concerning which he wrote to the Rev. John Telford.

THE DREAM OF GERONTIUS

It was indeed a great sight that he *saw*, and saw in sleep. For the word " sleeper " is emphatic, and also we read " Perhaps something *woke* him."

But if this dream was an inspiration there may be said to have been, as regards the poem, a double inspiration, for Newman undoubtedly spoke as if his writing down of what he had dreamt or seen came through some agency other than his own volition. He wrote to Mr. Allies in October, 1865, and said " it came into my head to write it. I really can't tell how . . . and I could no more write anything else by willing it than I could fly." It would seem that here he spoke rather of the " sudden inspiration," as Wilfrid Ward writes, which suddenly inspired him to preserve the dream in writing than of any inspired expression in which to do so. Certainly there was no irresistible torrent of verbal inspiration, for the small bits of paper—as far as they have been put before us in facsimile—contain much of alteration and correction. Furthermore, even the " fair copy on foolscap " has its alterations and corrections, its two versions of the Psalm chanted by the Souls in Purgatory, and a hymn which never was to be printed with the poem. Nor did these alterations and corrections cease with the fair copy on foolscap. What " came into my head," on January 17th, 1865, was " to write it," not immediately and precisely the words in which to do so. At the same time we are to understand that the writing was no more

16

a matter entirely of Newman's own volition or " willing "
than had been his dreaming of the dream which that
writing described and preserved. For he spoke, in the
Telford letter, of the " protection and pattern " of
" various spiritual writers." He says " under their protection and pattern I have set down the dream as it
came before the sleeper "—i.e. under the protection and
pattern of various "spiritual writers." This "protection"
and " pattern " may account for those resemblances (to
give two instances) to Dante and Calderon which have
so frequently been found in the poem.

It speaks well for the critical insight of Sir Francis
Doyle that many years before these letters were made
public he should have thought of Newman as of one
who should be " united to the rapt singers and prophets
of old by links of feeling, and touches of privilege, which
obtain no entrance into more brilliant souls ; " and, he
went on to say, " it is not wonderful, therefore, if we
pause sometimes to consider whether it be not to such
as him, rather than to such as them, that we ought to
look for any last fragments of the lost and forgotten tune,
for any last faint echoes upon earth from that primeval
melody which arose in heaven when ' the morning stars
sang together, and all the sons of God shouted for joy.' "
And again Doyle's account of the poem as " springing
up spontaneously out of the innermost fountains of a
deeply religious mind " may be regarded as a not alto-

gether infelicitous way of saying " it came into my head to write it," and, " I have said what I saw." One of the most interesting revelations to be gathered from the Telford letter is that the title of the poem was a plain statement of a plain fact. The dream of Gerontius was the dream Gerontius dreamt, the dream that an " old man " dreamt—an " old man " whose name was Newman.

It is a strange story ; this story of the coming and of the writing down of the dream. And surely not the least strange part of it is, that, after such an experience, after having dreamt it, after his " sudden inspiration " to set it down in the shape of a dramatic poem, after the " protection and pattern " of " various spiritual writers " had been vouchsafed to him as he wrote it down on fifty-two small bits of paper—that after all this he should have " forgotten it," forgotten it not after many years but after only not very many weeks ! Yet to such a strange forgetfulness do Newman's own words testify.

The manuscript, whether rough or fair or both (for the " fair copy on foolscap " begins with the date January 17th, and ends with that of February 1st), was put into one of what the poet called his " pigeon-holes," and, had it not been for the " accident to which we now pass," it might have remained " forgotten " there for who shall say how long ?

INTRODUCTION

The Wise Editor " The wise editor," wrote Aubrey de Vere, " did care, and it was published at once."

Who was this wise editor, and what was the " magazine " which he wisely edited ? Bellasis informs us that the MS. was sent "to Fr. Coleridge, S.J., editor of the *Month*, and appeared in two portions, in successive numbers of that periodical (April, May, 1865)."

And yet here we come upon what at first sight might seem to be a discrepancy.

For the *Month* itself, in an article signed with the initials J. G. (December, 1902), speaks of Father H. J. Coleridge " becoming the Editor " at a later date than April and May, 1865,—" when in the middle of 1865 " (J. G. also states) " the Magazine changed hands, sundry alterations were introduced. Father Coleridge, who became editor, remodelled things considerably." And we are told that the " first number " which appeared after Father Coleridge " became editor " was " that for July, 1865." How then can Father Coleridge have been editor in the April and May of that year ?

The key to whatever difficulty there may be lies in that " changed hands." What seems to have happened was that when the Jesuit Fathers " took over " (J. G.) the *Month* in the middle of 1865 they officially appointed Father Coleridge editor. That is to say, the new management appointed for their editor him who had been editor under the old. They may be said to have re-

19

appointed him. That he had been editor before July, 1865, is quite certain. Not only is there the not to be gainsaid statement of Bellasis, but some of Newman's letters to Father Coleridge have been published, letters dated as early as May and June, 1865, and plainly and evidently written to one who was editor of the *Month*, —not to the editor yet officially appointed by the new management but still to him whom the new management were to continue in his editing.

The matter is not without its importance, because of the so deep a debt of gratitude that is owed to him who may be said to have discovered, or to have caused to be discovered, the poem. It is a pleasure to be able to chronicle his name. The *Month* has itself said (December, 1902), that "it is undoubtedly the greatest distinction of which *The Month* can boast that the 'Dream of Gerontius' made its first appearance in its pages." And that the poem did so make its first appearance in its pages can be traced to the wise importunity of Father Coleridge. Wherefore let his memory be accorded its due meed of honour and gratitude by all lovers of literature.

The present writer counts himself happy in the possession of a perfect set of the lemony-covered numbers of the *Month* for 1865. The number in which the First Part of the poem appeared was No. XI. of Vol. II. That number was illustrated by two specimens of the

black and white art of Walter Crane, and contained
eight contributions though only seven contributors, for
two of the contributions were from Dr. Newman. Both
of these were signed " J. H. N.," although in the " Contents " those much-signifying initials were, for whatever
reason, only given to the former of the two contributions,
that one being described as " *The Dream of Gerontius.
By J. H. N.*" The *Dream* was given the third place
amongst the contents, and extended from page 415 to
page 425.

In the June number

> *The Dream of Gerontius.* By J. H. N. (concluded)

was placed second of the seven contributions, and went
from page 532 to page 544. Whether designedly or by
accident the

> But hark ! upon my sense
> Comes a fierce hubbub, which would make me fear,
> Could I be frighted.

which had brought Part I. to an end reappears in the
June number and makes the beginning of Part II.

The wording of the poem in these two parts was not
perfectly identical with the First Edition of its appearance as a book. Of the alterations the most important
was to be the changing of

> Softly and gently, dearest, sweetest soul,

to

> Softly and gently, dearly-ransomed soul.

THE DREAM OF GERONTIUS

There was to be another alteration of

> a deep, mysterious harmony :

to

> a grand, mysterious harmony :

And there were to be some other minor differences. Thus l. 720 now begins with " And," whereas the *Month* began with " Not." The *Month* gave

> Has but the brutes for kin,

instead of

> Had but the brutes for kin.

And at l. 656 the " old " of the *Month* was to become " eld." A very nice commentator might note that the " passed " of l. 381 was to be subsequently altered to " past," as " coulds't " was to appear at l. 732 instead of " couldest." The hyphen of " Vice-roy " was also doomed to disappear.

Some might even think it worth while to point out that the passage which begins

> Rescue him, O Lord, in this his evil hour,

appeared in the magazine with no *Amen* bracketed, and that ll. 564–566 were therein thus printed—

> All thou hast lost, new-made and glorified—
> —How, even now, the consummated Saints
> See God in heaven ; I may not explicate :—

22

INTRODUCTION

There were also certain differences of form, that is to say, that the *Month* printed the Chorus of Demons after a fashion never since followed, and that the Five Hymns of Praise of the Choirs of Angelicals were presented in the shape of couplets, although what we now know as the second and third lines of quatrains all began with capital letters.

There are various differences between the printed poem in the *Month* and the " fair copy on foolscap " reproduced in the *Complete Facsimile of the Original Fair Copy and of Portions of the First Rough Draft* (Longmans), which has the *Memorandum* of Bellasis.

The reason of these variations is to be found in the MS. of the *Dream* in the British Museum, the copied MS. which " was sent with autograph corrections to Fr. Coleridge, S.J." (Bellasis.)

Few must be the great poems whose appearance in manuscript may be as easily studied as may that of the *Dream*. Bellasis writes: " There are two manuscripts of the poem. The first, with repetitions, corrections, and erasures, is on fifty-two scraps of paper." And of the second manuscript he says that it is " a fair copy on foolscap with further corrections and erasures." This is the manuscript which his *Facsimile* may be said to have made accessible to the world at large, as it also makes accessible eight specimens of the first manuscript's fifty-two scraps of paper.

THE DREAM OF GERONTIUS

But the "copy of the *Dream*, not holographic, now in the British Museum," to which Bellasis alludes in his *Memorandum*, has an interest of its own, and a considerable one, for from its pages was printed the *Dream* as it appeared originally in the *Month*. It is catalogued, at the British Museum, as :—

"*Newman* (John Henry) *Cardinal. The Dream of Gerontius*, circ. 1865. Partly *autogr.*"

There has been added to the copy a prefatory statement which runs :—

Purch^d of Miss F M. Taylor,
16 March, 1891 :

which addition has been followed by another in these words :—

The original M S of
Dream of Gerontius by Cardinal Newman
contains twenty-nine pages
given by the Cardinal to the present owner
F. M. Taylor The Convent Brentford
Price one hundred pounds.

The "original M S" must evidently mean here only the original MS. from which the *Dream* was printed.

The "copy," to which the above statements are now attached, is written in a fair, clerkly hand, the First

INTRODUCTION

Part of the poem being transcribed on white blue-lined foolscap, while for the Second Part the copyist used blue foolscap. The pages are frequently marked with pencilled instructions to printers, such as : " Observe the indentations," " Follow the indentation," and " Indent deeper." There is such an " observe the indentation " to the first song of the Angel, and Newman has a " To the Printer, J. H. N." on p. 9. The pencil has also preserved the names of several compositors. The identity, in the copy, of the close of Part I with the opening of Part II. has been observed by someone—perhaps by Father Coleridge—for against the first verses of Part II. is written " is this to be repeated ? " a question which, as the event was to show, was to be answered, for whatever reason, in the affirmative. The most interesting of the corrections in Newman's own handwriting is at what, owing to the introduction of the insertion, is become p. 19 of the copy. On a small piece of paper the poet wrote :—

" Dr Newman wishes Messrs Robson to be so good as to insert two lines as below, into the *Dream of Gerontius*,

after

' All thou hast lost, new made and glorified,'

these two

How even now, the consummated Saints
See God in heaven, I may not tell to thee."

THE DREAM OF GERONTIUS

The last line of the above must have received some later re-correction, for in the *Month* the verse appeared as :—

See God in heaven, I may not explicate.

In the above insertion, and in an autograph " J. H. N." which attests authorship, there is perhaps sufficient justification for the " Partly autogr." of the Catalogue. The First Part of the poem bears the Birmingham post-mark, which seems to speak of no very careful preparation for its passage through the post.

It is noticeable that the one solitary stage-direction (if it may be so called) of the poem disappeared, by erasure, amongst the " autograph corrections." In the " original Fair Copy " there was written

(A pause)

between the ending

Christ, our Lord ;

of the Priest's prayer and the noble passage which begins with the departed Soul's

I went to sleep ; and now I am refreshed,—.

Before we leave the *Month* it is as well to make a note of the fact that in the " Contents " of Vol. II. which was inserted between page 572 and page 573 of the June number, 1865, there was plainly printed

Dream of Gerontius. By Dr. Newman 415, 532.

INTRODUCTION

The poem and the statement as to its authorship were re-echoed in the *Catholic World*, a monthly magazine published in New York which described itself as " Eclectic," and not without good reason. For in July and August, 1865, the *Catholic World* reproduced the two parts of the *Dream* of the *Month* with such conscientious exactitude that the lines

> But hark ! upon my sense
> Comes a fierce hubbub, which would make me fear,
> Could I be frighted.

were again printed in both parts. The *Dream* of the *Catholic World* differed only from that of the *Month* in this—that it was headed :—

> From *The Month*.   By John Henry Newman, D.D.

The Book We are not only indebted to Father Coleridge for the result of his request on behalf of his magazine, but also for his suggestion to the contributor of the *Dream* that he should publish the poem separately in the form of a book.   There is a letter to " My dear Fr. Coleridge," and dated November 22nd, 1865, in which Newman said: " I am taking your suggestion and publishing Gerontius."   When in October, 1900, the *Dream* of Sir Edward Elgar was to be for the first time performed at the Birmingham Musical Festival the writer of the " Occasional Notes " of the *Musical Times* contributed to that publication the following note of occasion :—

"It is stated in the usually accurate *Julian's Dictionary*, that the poem was first published in Newman's *Verses on Various Occasions*, in the year 1868. *The Dream of Gerontius* made its first appearance separately, in a 32mo booklet of fifty-five pages, published at sixpence by Messrs. Burns, Lambert and Oates, three years earlier, i.e. in 1865."

Here the corrector of Dr. Julian stands himself in need of correction. For the 32mo booklet was published not in 1865, but one year later, i.e. in 1866. Curiously enough no less a personage than Newman's chief,—or perhaps one should say only—biographer has fallen into the same mistake.

"The poem appeared in the Jesuit periodical, the *Month*, then edited by his friend, Father Coleridge, in the numbers for April and May. When it was republished in November, etc." (Ward's *Life*).

The great lexicographer of the *Dictionary of Hymnology* was to profit by the correction in the *Musical Times*. In the New Supplement to his Revised Edition of 1907 he most accurately noted: "A copy of the rare first separate edition of the *Dream* (1866) is in the Brit. Mus. and another in the Church House, Westminster."

INTRODUCTION

Perhaps the present writer may be allowed to state here that yet another is in the room in which he is writing. There is nothing to add to the accurate description of the little book which we have seen in the *Musical Times*, beyond possibly that the colour of its binding is some sort of a brown. The copy now before the writer is greatly enriched by reason of its being a Presentation Copy, having written just before the Dedication (which now appeared for the first time) the following inscription :—

M. J. Rhodes,
With the author's kind regards.

April 21, 1866.

Mr. Gladstone, twenty-two years after this publication of the book said, in a letter to Mr. Lawrence Dillon, of the poem, " It originally came into the world in grave clothes ; swaddled, that is to say, in the folds of the anonymous, but it has now fairly burst them, and will, I hope, take and hold its position as literature of the world." This was a highly characteristic way of stating that the *Dream* had been published with no author's name upon the title-page. But while that was true, the book can scarcely be said to have been published with an anonymity which was anonymous. For there was a " J. H. N." set below the Dedication, and surely most people in 1866—when Newman was in his sixty-sixth year—could have had but little difficulty about knowing what " J. H. N." stood for, especially when those initials were attached to such a Dedication, and to the Dedication of such a poem. Moreover, as we have already noted, the " Contents " of Vol. II. of the *Month* had plainly printed " Dream of Gerontius. By Dr. Newman." Though indeed the advertised statement in the *Month* that it contained contributions by the " Very Rev. Dr. Newman " would surely of itself have been a very clear interpretation of the " J. H. N." So that why Gladstone should have thought, as late as 1888, that the little book had " now fairly burst " " the folds of the anonymous " is a little hard to understand.

Perhaps one may say that the poem was published as a book without any author's name, and yet many must have known very well what the author's name was— that the initials were equivalent to the full signature. Certainly all readers of the *Month* knew, for they had been told, as had been told also the readers of the American *Catholic World.* That Newman himself was not the least anxious to keep on whatever mockery of mask the " J. H. N." may have made for him is much evident by the plain fact that " with the author's kind regards " was, in April, 1866, written in his own handwriting.

INTRODUCTION

Those who listened, forty-seven years ago, at Oxford, to the Lectures of that University's Professor of Poetry, went away from one of them having learnt that " Gerontius is meant to be studied and dwelt upon by the meditative reader." For the sake of any who like to be aided in their studies by the writings of those who by the polite world have been held worthy of helping their fellow-readers, I will here give, although to do so is only to recapitulate, some of their names who have written directly upon the *Dream.*

Sir Francis Doyle (Lectures delivered before the University of Oxford, 1868), H. J. Jennings (*Cardinal Newman*), Alfred Austin (*The Poetry of the Period*), R. H. Hutton (*Cardinal Newman*), Dr. William Barry (*Newman*), William Stebbing (*The Poets: Geoffrey Chaucer to Alfred Tennyson*), and William E. A. Axon ("The Dream of Gerontius," *The Library*, 1908), A. R. Waller and G. H. S. Burrow (*John Henry, Cardinal Newman*), have all dealt in particular with the poem. Mr. Henri Bremond (*The Mystery of Newman*) has many important references to it and to its text.

An Annotated Edition of the poem has been published by Longmans, of which the annotator is Professor Maurice Francis Egan. His scientific metrical or pro-sodial study of the verse is of great value, and might give to many a nearly new interpretation of the poem.

The French versions have acute Prefaces (Trebutien, Lebourg).

31

But as an interpretation of the poem the music of Sir Edward Elgar has a place peculiar to itself, and is criticism of a kind other, and higher, than that which any prose can claim to be. Of Elgar's music one critical and descriptive analysis has been written by A. J. Jeager (Novello) and another by Ernest Newman (John Lane). The "meditative reader," even the meditative reader who is not musical, will find both of these studies not less useful than delightful.

Ward's *Life*, and the *Introduction* and *Memorandum* of Bellasis, possess, of course, attributes of authority such as are possessed by nothing else.

In the Annotated Edition to which reference has been made Professor Egan limited the number of his " Notes " to twelve. Any would-be annotator could easily reap from the harvest-fields that only I have mentioned a wondrous harvest of notes. And were such to stray further amongst the occasional allusions to the poem which stand so thickly about the prairies of print no doubt he or she could easily garner another. I imagine him or her eagerly transcribing (for instance) the remarks of Hutton which are to be found beyond the boundary of that book of his that I have named, and copying with zest the superlatively kind things that Swinburne had to say of the " rhymed or rhymeless iambics—as here and there in *The Dream of Gerontius* " in the *Nineteenth Century* for May, 1884. Nor would these chiels neglect to note that Andrew Lang, in his *History of English Literature*, pronounced that "*The Dream of Gerontius* displays intense imaginative power." And there is another rich armful waiting for the carrying-away in the *Cardinal Newman's Course* of Dean Church.

Much indeed of like spoil could my reaper bring back from his search, but surely nothing that would be of more interest than the following extract from a letter written by Charles Kingsley in May, 1868, to Sir William Cope, and printed in Vol. II. of the *Charles Kingsley* which was edited by his widow.

" I find that your Newman's poems have been returned without my expressing my opinion of the *Dream of Gerontius*. I read the *Dream* with awe and admiration. However utterly I may differ from the *entourage* in which Dr. Newman's present creed surrounds the central idea, I must feel that that central idea is as true as it is noble, and it, as I suppose, is this: The longing of the soul to behold Deity, converted by the mere act of sight, into a self-abasement and self-annihilation so utter, that the soul is ready, even glad, to be hurled back to any depth, to endure any pain, from the moment that it becomes aware of God's actual perfection and its own utter impurity and meanness.

" How poor my words are in expressing what Dr. N. has exprest in poetry, I am well aware. But I am thankful to any man, who under any parabolic, or even questionably true forms, will teach that to a generation which is losing more and more the sense of reverence, and beginning confessedly to hate excellence for its own sake, as the Greek ostracised Aristides, because he was tired of hearing him called the Just. As for the mocking of the fiends, I did not feel with the Bishop of Oxford that it indicated any possibility of unbelief, but rather showed merely that Dr. N. had looked fairly at the other side of a great question, and dare say the worst which can be said on it, which he would not have dared to do, had he not made up his mind."

That is not only interesting criticism, but illuminative, and not only illuminative but generous. A less large-hearted man than Kingsley might not have so completely remembered not past years—years which, in 1868, were only just past.

I would here state that all study of the *Dream* should be accompanied by study of the *Apologia*, and of many of the letters, and much of the matter other than letters, of Wilfrid Ward's *Life*.

There is much evidence to prove that readers of poetry like to know how their poets look or have looked. Of portraits, and of reproductions of portraits, of John Henry Newman there is assuredly no lack. From a literary point of view not one of them all is more interesting than the one contributed by Thackeray to *Punch* (Vol. XIX, p. 243, 1850). In the accompanying letterpress the subject of the artist is called " Mr. Newboy." It is not probable that Dr. Newman sat to Mr. Thackeray for this portrait, and there have been critics of Thackeray as an artist who might have said that it would not have made much difference if many sittings had been given. The thing is a caricature, but it is evident that Thackeray was not unacquainted with the features of " Mr. Newboy," though the interest attached to the drawing is chiefly literary. Nevertheless from any monograph dealing with the Portraits of Newman mention of this characteristic example of Thackeray's drawing ought not to be omitted.

Newman and "Nature" It is scarcely for me to traverse any of the opinions of those to whose names and works I have made reference. But I may perhaps be allowed a word or two upon Sir Francis Doyle's remarks on Newman's attitude towards what is often called " nature." Doyle seems to have found Newman " somewhat hard and cold to the beauty of the outer world." And Aubrey de Vere wrote: " I remember urging him to make an expedition with me, when I was well enough, amid the beautiful scenery of Wicklow, and his answering with a smile that life was full of work more important than the enjoyment of mountains and lakes."

One must suppose that that to which Doyle found

Newman " somewhat hard and cold " was that side of things which had to do with mountains and lakes. Yet to " the beauty of the outer world " Newman was certainly neither hard nor cold. No one could doubt that who had read no more than

> There stray'd awhile, amid the woods of Dart
> One who could love them, but who durst not love.

But Newman had his own way of regarding " nature," and it was a way which only his own extraordinary command of the English language could express—and did express, as all students of his writings very well know. Hutton has on this subject a sentence of much fine gold ; " He has always been disposed to regard the material world as a mere hieroglyphic expression of deeper spiritual meanings." With Newman it was always so.

The snapdragon on the wall of Trinity was a snapdragon to him and it was something very much more. The moor and fen, the crag and torrent were to Newman by no means only moors and fens, and crags and torrents. Doyle said that he thought that Newman " scarce believes in any real rose, in any actual rainbow." One can imagine Sir Francis inviting Newman to come and enjoy the rainbow and the rose, just as one can fancy Newman replying to him with that same smile with which he had replied to Aubrey de Vere, with the smile of deeper spiritual meanings than most smiles may be supposed to have. But it is hard to understand how anybody who had studied the *Dream* with a view to lecturing upon it at Oxford could have found its author hard and cold to the beauty of the outer world. One wonders how anyone could think so who had read such a passage as this :—

> The sound is like the rushing of the wind—
> The summer wind among the lofty pines ;
> Swelling and dying, echoing round about,
> Now here, now distant, wild and beautiful ;
> While, scattered from the branches it has stirred,
> Descend ecstatic odours.

But what one notices in the above is that when he heard the angels singing he heard also the wind in the pines, just as (one perceives) when he had heard the wind in the pines he had heard also the singing of the angels. In the same way, as he nears that high place where

> A band of mighty Angels keep the way
> On either side, and hymn the Incarnate God,

does Gerontius say of the " grand mysterious harmony " that

> It floods me, like the deep and solemn sound
> Of many waters.

So surely was Newman wont to hear in the deep and solemn sound of many waters the grand mysterious harmony of the mighty Angels of the Sacred Stair.

37

THE DREAM OF GERONTIUS

Newman must always be for us associated with light. He makes the Guardian Angel of the poem say :—

> By sun and moon, primeval ordinances—
> By stars which rise and set harmoniously—
> By the recurring seasons,—

and the lines remind us of those of Æschylus (or of Æschylus as blacksmithed out on the anvil of Browning) which he puts into the mouth of his watcher for the " glow of fire "—

> I know of nightly star-groups the assemblage,
> And those that bring to men winter and summer,
> Bright dynasts, as they pride them in the æther
> —Stars, when they wither, and the uprisings of them.

So was Newman also a watcher for " the torch's token." Did he not call one of his poems *The Watchman*, and another *The Watch by Night*, and another *Waiting for the Morning* ? And it is far from easy to say where there is in poetry a more perfect suggestion of the coming of the morning than in one of the simple stanzas of the Hymn, the *Dream's* Third Choir of Angelicals—

> But to the younger race there rose
> A hope upon its fall ;
> And slowly, surely, gracefully,
> The morning dawned on all.

Of course there is here, as everywhere, the Huttonian " hieroglyphic expression of deeper spiritual meanings." But because Newman could unriddle the meaning of the hieroglyph it is by no means necessary to believe that he could not also feel its beauty. Such references as the *Dream* has to " nature " would seem to make it evident that he did. After all he did not disparage the beauty of mountains and lakes to Aubrey de Vere—indeed he used the word " enjoyment." But doubtless his own enjoyment of mountains and lakes is to be found intertwined with such lines as

> And may thy place to-day be found in peace,
> And may thy dwelling be the Holy Mount
> Of Sion :

and

> And carefully I dip thee in the lake.

We find mention in the *Dream* of the " fragrant flower," of the " giants of the wood," of the " tempest's din," of the " lightning-flash," of " the seaside cave," and of the "face of day," but it is evident that upon each of these examples of " the beauty of the outward world " had looked that spiritual-specialist's eye which one may be pardoned for sometimes thinking entitled Newman to number himself with his Angel's

> Us of the immaterial world.

After Fifty Years *The Dream of Gerontius* which, as we have seen, was published as a contribution to a magazine in 1865 and as a book in 1866, soon got itself read. The *Spectator* reviewed it in March, 1866. Doyle was lecturing upon it at Oxford in 1868, and found himself at that time able to say to his audience " I can hardly doubt that every one of you is at least as well acquainted with it as I am myself," and he himself was very well acquainted with it. In the same year— the year of *Verses on Various Occasions*—the critic of the *Athenæum* stated that it was " a work of much intellectual power." In 1868 also Sir William Cope was lending it to Kingsley, and Kingsley and the then Bishop of Oxford were in disagreement about the Demons. And in 1868 the Hymn of the Fifth Choir of Angelicals was to be found amongst those of *Hymns Ancient and Modern*. Alfred Austin was writing about it in *Temple Bar* in 1869, and informing his readers that "we have here a very beautiful and very complete poem." In 1869, also, a French translation appeared. In January, 1876, the Rev. H. N. Oxenham was quoting, in the *Contemporary Review*, from " Dr. Newman's masterly poem, *The Dream of Gerontius*," and saying that " the poem is in everybody's hands." And although we only hear of Gladstone speaking about the poem in 1879 it is more than probable that he had long before that spoken of the *Dream* " in the same breath with the *Divina Commedia*." Edition succeeded to edition, and I find that one which is dated with the same year in which Sir M. E. Grant Duff recorded in his Diary the enthusiasm of Gladstone is described as the " Fourteenth Edition."

For fifty years the number of the poem's readers' has

steadily grown, without hurry and without pause, and
this continuous growth has been the sign of life. It was
not a poem written for a generation, it has had about it
nothing whatsoever of the fireworks of fashion, neither
has its constant advance at any time been hastened
with that supreme form of advertisement which is known
as a boom.

Dr. Alexander Whyte, lecturing to his Scottish
students, said to them : " It is a poem that every man
should have by heart who has it before him to die."
This was equivalent to saying that everybody ought to
know *The Dream of Gerontius* by heart. To hope for
such a consummation is certainly to nourish the larger
hope, or the largest hope, but somehow that hope does
not seem so extravagant and wild as would be the one
that everybody should have the works of some other
mentionable poets by heart—even their chief works.

If amongst contemporary poems the *Dream* was
" unique " the reason for it being so would seem to have
been that amongst contemporary poets its writer was
unique. Doyle said of him—

" If, then, at such moments we find in our path some
lonely and single-minded searcher after wisdom—

' Whose soul is like a star, and dwells apart '—

if we find one for whom life is no arena upon which
brilliant accomplishments may be displayed, or glittering

crowns of victory arrived at—no place for easy pleasure, or even the most innocent self-indulgence, we are surprised and startled into reverence."

So Doyle spoke of Newman in 1868—of whom else amongst the poets of that time could he have so spoken ?

Whether Newman was a better or greater man than his contemporaries in poetry, or a better or greater poet, are questions which no umpire exists finally to decide. But it needs no umpire to tell us that he was a different man, and a different poet. It may be that those others, as he, said what they saw, but they did not see what he did and so could not say what he said.

Everyone knows that Gordon, when for him the transitory was about to collapse, read, and marked, *The Dream of Gerontius.* Everybody has heard that the last hours of Gladstone were comforted by its pages. And Wilfrid Ward quotes one who said " I knew a poor stocking-weaver who on his death-bed made his wife read it to him continually. Grant Duff has chronicled the fact that the Rev. H. N. Oxenham " had the *Dream of Gerontius* read to him as the end drew near." Oxenham and Gladstone and the poor stocking-weaver would have all understood that saying of Dr. Alexander Whyte. Just as Gordon would have understood it. Of Gordon Newman himself wrote : " What struck me so much in his use of the *Dream* was that in St. Paul's words he 'died daily'; he was always on his death-bed, fulfilling the common advice that we should ever pass the day as if it were our last." *He was always on his death-bed.* And who is not always on his death-bed ?

> Pallida Mors aequo pulsat pede pauperum tabernas
> Regumque turres.

And one may surely see one of Newman's Horatian echoes or memories in the

> a visitant
> Is knocking his dire summons at my door,—

of the *Dream.*

The words "I am near to death" end the first verse of the poem, and the last word of its last line is "morrow." That it is so must remind us how to the phrase "for to-morrow we die" can be given either of two interpretations. We are apt to associate one of those meanings with certain Corinthian Greeks and with a certain English Persian. But what these appear to have understood by the words was not the meaning that they held for the author of *The Dream of Gerontius*—for him who heard the Soul's

> I hear the voices that I left on earth,

even as the great Angel of the Agony was beginning his solemn pleading before the Throne of God.

As I bring to a close my little hoard of gleanings there

reaches me a report of the Sermon Preached by the Archbishop of Canterbury on the evening of Sunday, January 3rd, 1915, the day appointed for the Intercession of the Allied Nations. " We feel " (so I find his Grace saying) " how the very passing of those brave and buoyant lives into the world beyond pierces the flimsy barrier between the things which are seen and temporal and the things which are unseen and eternal, and again we give thanks."

As all of us may also give thanks for him who in another sense and in another way once pierced that flimsy barrier, and who, when questioned upon the great poem of which such piercing was the cause, answered with convincing simplicity : *I have said what I saw.*

The
Illustra-
tions
And since he set down faithfully what he saw it almost necessarily follows that for the majority of his readers a veil was lifted and some measure of the seer's gift imparted to them. To certain of such readers it has been granted, in greater or less degree, to report their experience. And here one thinks at once of Elgar and his music. And here, also, one must now think of the art of Stella Langdale. Let me now but say of her work that it has plainly behind it and beneath it a spirit to whose deep another deep has called, a spirit that has succeeded in passing on the message. For that the message has been clearly

INTRODUCTION

heard and truthfully transmitted any serious study of her translation of her text immediately makes evident. This is as it should be. The unique poem demands the unique interpreter, and even thus highly qualified may be the pictorial commentator of the following pages.

GORDON TIDY

THE DREAM OF GERONTIUS

THE DREAM OF GERONTIUS

GERONTIUS

ESU, MARIA—I am near to death,
    And Thou art calling me; I know it now—
Not by the token of this faltering breath,
    This chill at heart, this dampness on my
        brow,
(Jesu, have mercy! Mary, pray for me!)—
   'Tis this new feeling, never felt before,
(Be with me, Lord, in my extremity!)
    That I am going, that I am no more.
'Tis this strange innermost abandonment,
    (Lover of souls! great God! I look to Thee,)
This emptying out of each constituent
    And natural force, by which I come to be.
Pray for me, O my friends; a visitant
    Is knocking his dire summons at my door,
The like of whom, to scare me and to daunt,
    Has never, never come to me before;

THE DREAM OF GERONTIUS

'Tis death, — O loving friends, your prayers ! — 'tis
    he ! . . . .
  As though my very being had given way,
  As though I was no more a substance now,
And could fall back on nought to be my stay,   ·
  (Help, loving Lord ! Thou my sole Refuge, Thou,)
And turn no whither, but must needs decay
  And drop from out the universal frame
Into that shapeless, scopeless, blank abyss,
  That utter nothingness, of which I came :
This is it that has come to pass in me ;
O horror ! this it is, my dearest, this ;
So pray for me, my friends, who have not strength
    to pray.

ASSISTANTS

    Kyrie eleïson, Christe eleïson, Kyrie eleison.
    Holy Mary, pray for him.
    All holy Angels, pray for him.
    Choirs of the righteous, pray for him.
    Holy Abraham, pray for him.
    St. John Baptist, St. Joseph, pray for him.
    St. Peter, St. Paul, St. Andrew, St. John,
    All Apostles, all Evangelists, pray for him.

Into that shapeless, scopeless, blank abyss,
That utter nothingness, of which I came.

THE DREAM OF GERONTIUS

All holy Disciples of the Lord, pray for him.
All holy Innocents, pray for him.
All holy Martyrs, all holy Confessors,
All holy Hermits, all holy Virgins,
All ye Saints of God, pray for him.

GERONTIUS

Rouse thee, my fainting soul, and play the man ;
    And through such waning span
Of life and thought as still has to be trod,
    Prepare to meet thy God.
And while the storm of that bewilderment
    Is for a season spent,
And, ere afresh the ruin on thee fall,
    Use well the interval.

ASSISTANTS

Be merciful, be gracious ; spare him, Lord.
Be merciful, be gracious ; Lord, deliver him.
    From the sins that are past ;
        From Thy frown and Thine ire ;
            From the perils of dying ;
            From any complying
            With sin, or denying

THE DREAM OF GERONTIUS

His God, or relying
On self, at the last ;
   From the nethermost fire ;
From all that is evil ;
From power of the devil ;
Thy servant deliver,
For once and for ever.

By Thy birth, and by Thy Cross,
Rescue him from endless loss ;
By Thy death and burial,
Save him from a final fall ;
By Thy rising from the tomb,
   By Thy mounting up above,
   By the Spirit's gracious love,
Save him in the day of doom.

GERONTIUS

Sanctus fortis, Sanctus Deus,
   De profundis oro te,
Miserere, Judex meus,
   Parce mihi, Domine.
Firmly I believe and truly
   God is Three, and God is One ;

And I next acknowledge duly
  Manhood taken by the Son.
And I trust and hope most fully
  In that Manhood crucified ;
And each thought and deed unruly
  Do to death, as He has died.
Simply to His grace and wholly
  Light and life and strength belong,
And I love, supremely, solely,
  Him the holy, Him the strong.
Sanctus fortis, Sanctus Deus,
  De profundis oro te,
Miserere, Judex meus,
  Parce mihi, Domine.
And I hold in veneration,
  For the love of Him alone,
Holy Church, as His creation,
  And her teachings, as His own.
And I take with joy whatever
  Now besets me, pain or fear,
And with a strong will I sever
  All the ties which bind me here.
Adoration aye be given,
  With and through the angelic host,

THE DREAM OF GERONTIUS

To the God of earth and heaven,
  Father, Son, and Holy Ghost.
Sanctus fortis, Sanctus Deus,
  De profundis oro te,
Miserere, Judex meus,
  Mortis in discrimine.

I can no more ; for now it comes again,
That sense of ruin, which is worse than pain,
That masterful negation and collapse
Of all that makes me man ; as though I bent
Over the dizzy brink
Of some sheer infinite descent ;
Or worse, as though
Down, down for ever I was falling through
The solid framework of created things,
And needs must sink and sink
Into the vast abyss. And, crueller still,
A fierce and restless fright begins to fill
The mansion of my soul. And, worse and worse,
Some bodily form of ill
Floats on the wind, with many a loathsome curse
Tainting the hallowed air, and laughs, and flaps
Its hideous wings,

And makes me wild with horror and dismay.

O Jesu, help ! pray for me, Mary, pray !

Some angel, Jesu ! such as came to Thee

In Thine own agony. . . . .

Mary, pray for me. Joseph, pray for me. Mary, pray
    for me.

ASSISTANTS

Rescue him, O Lord, in this his evil hour,

As of old so many by Thy gracious power :—(Amen.)

Enoch and Elias from the common doom ; (Amen.)

Noe from the waters in a saving home ; (Amen.)

Abraham from th' abounding guilt of Heathenesse ; (Amen.)

Job from all his multiform and fell distress ; (Amen.)

Isaac, when his father's knife was raised to slay ; (Amen.)

Lot from burning Sodom on its judgment-day ; (Amen.)

Moses from the land of bondage and despair ; (Amen.)

Daniel from the hungry lions in their lair ; (Amen.)

And the Children Three amid the furnace-flame ; (Amen.)

Chaste Susanna from the slander and the shame ; (Amen.)

David from Golia and the wrath of Saul ; (Amen.)

And the two Apostles from their prison-thrall ; (Amen.)

Thecla from her torments ; (Amen.)

        —so, to show Thy power,

Rescue this Thy servant in his evil hour.

THE DREAM OF GERONTIUS

GERONTIUS

Novissima hora est ; and I fain would sleep ;
The pain has wearied me. . . . Into Thy hands,
O Lord, into Thy hands . . .

THE PRIEST

Proficiscere, anima Christiana, de hoc mundo !
Go forth upon thy journey, Christian soul !
Go from this world ! Go, in the name of God
The omnipotent Father, who created thee !
Go, in the name of Jesus Christ, our Lord,
Son of the living God, who bled for thee !
Go, in the name of the Holy Spirit, who
Hath been poured out on thee ! Go, in the name
Of Angels and Archangels ; in the name
Of Thrones and Dominations ; in the name
Of Princedoms and of Powers ; and in the name
Of Cherubim and Seraphim, go forth !
Go, in the name of Patriarchs and Prophets ;
And of Apostles and Evangelists,
Of Martyrs and Confessors ; in the name
Of holy Monks and Hermits ; in the name
Of holy Virgins ; and all Saints of God,
Both men and women, go ! Go on thy course !

56

Go forth upon thy journey, Christian soul !
Go from this world !

And may thy place to-day be found in peace,
And may thy dwelling be the Holy Mount
Of Sion :—in the name of Christ, our Lord.

II

SOUL OF GERONTIUS

I went to sleep ; and now I am refreshed.
A strange refreshment : for I feel in me
An inexpressive lightness, and a sense
Of freedom, as I were at length myself,
And ne'er had been before.   How still it is !
I hear no more the busy beat of time,
No, nor my fluttering breath, nor struggling pulse ;
Nor does one moment differ from the next.
I had a dream ; yes :—someone softly said
" He's gone " ; and then a sigh went round the room.
And then I surely heard a priestly voice
Cry " Subvenite " ; and they knelt in prayer.
I seem to hear him still ; but thin and low,
And fainter and more faint the accents come,
As at an ever-widening interval.
Ah ! whence is this ?   What is this severance ?
This silence pours a solitariness

Into the very essence of my soul,
And the deep rest, so soothing and so sweet,
Hath something too of sternness and of pain,
For it drives back my thoughts upon their spring
By a strange introversion, and perforce
I now begin to feed upon myself,
Because I have nought else to feed upon.

Am I alive or dead ? I am not dead,
But in the body still ; for I possess
A sort of confidence which clings to me,
That each particular organ holds its place
As heretofore, combining with the rest
Into one symmetry, that wraps me round,
And makes me man ; and surely I could move,
Did I but will it, every part of me.
And yet I cannot to my sense bring home,
By very trial, that I have the power.
'Tis strange ; I cannot stir a hand or foot,
I cannot make my fingers or my lips
By mutual pressure witness each to each,
Nor by the eyelid's instantaneous stroke
Assure myself I have a body still.
Nor do I know my very attitude,
Nor if I stand, or lie, or sit, or kneel.

THE DREAM OF GERONTIUS

So much I know, not knowing how I know,
That the vast universe, where I have dwelt,
Is quitting me, or I am quitting it.
Or I or it is rushing on the wings
Of light or lightning on an onward course,
And we e'en now are million miles apart.
Yet . . . is this peremptory severance
Wrought out in lengthening measurements of space,
Which grow and multiply by speed and time ?
Or am I traversing infinity
By endless subdivision, hurrying back
From finite towards infinitesimal,
Thus dying out of the expansed world ?

Another marvel ; someone has me fast
Within his ample palm ; 'tis not a grasp
Such as they use on earth, but all around
Over the surface of my subtle being,
As though I were a sphere, and capable
To be accosted thus, a uniform
And gentle pressure tells me I am not
Self-moving, but borne forward on my way.
And hark ! I hear a singing ; yet in sooth
I cannot of that music rightly say
Whether I hear or touch or taste the tones,
Oh what a heart-subduing melody !

THE DREAM OF GERONTIUS

My work is done,
My task is o'er,
And so I come,
Taking it home,
For the crown is won,
Alleluia,
For evermore.

My Father gave
In charge to me
This child of earth
E'en from its birth,
To serve and save,
Alleluia,
And saved is he.

This child of clay
To me was given,
To rear and train
By sorrow and pain
In the narrow way,
Alleluia,
From earth to heaven.

60

THE DREAM OF GERONTIUS

SOUL

It is a member of that family
Of wondrous beings, who, ere the worlds were made,
Millions of ages back, have stood around
The throne of God :—he never has known sin ;
But through those cycles all but infinite,
Has had a strong and pure celestial life,
And bore to gaze on th' unveiled face of God
And drank from the eternal Fount of truth,
And served Him with a keen ecstatic love.
Hark ! he begins again.

ANGEL

O Lord, how wonderful in depth and height,
    But most in man, how wonderful Thou art !
With what a love, what soft persuasive might
    Victorious o'er the stubborn fleshly heart,
  Thy tale complete of saints Thou dost provide,
  To fill the thrones which angels lost through pride !

He lay a grovelling babe upon the ground,
    Polluted in the blood of his first sire,
With his whole essence shattered and unsound,
    And, coiled around his heart, a demon dire,

Which was not of his nature, but had skill
To bind and form his opening mind to ill.

Then was I sent from heaven to set right
    The balance in his soul of truth and sin,
And I have waged a long relentless fight,
    Resolved that death-environed spirit to win,
    Which from its fallen state, when all was lost,
    Had been repurchased at so dread a cost.

Oh what a shifting parti-coloured scene
    Of hope and fear, of triumph and dismay,
Of recklessness and penitence, has been
    The history of that dreary, lifelong fray!
    And oh the grace to nerve him and to lead,
    How patient, prompt, and lavish at his need!

O man, strange composite of heaven and earth!
    Majesty dwarfed to baseness! fragrant flower
Running to poisonous seed! and seeming worth
    Cloking corruption! weakness mastering power!
    Who never art so near to crime and shame,
    As when thou hast achieved some deed of name;—

Then was I sent from Heaven to set right
The balance in his soul of truth and sin.

THE DREAM OF GERONTIUS

How should ethereal natures comprehend
    A thing made up of spirit and of clay,
Were we not tasked to nurse it and to tend,
     Linked one to one throughout its mortal day ?
   More than the Seraph in his height of place,
   The Angel-guardian knows and loves the ransomed race.

SOUL

Now know I surely that I am at length
Out of the body : had I part with earth,
I never could have drunk those accents in
And not have worshipped as a god the voice
That was so musical ; but now I am
So whole of heart, so calm, so self-possessed,
With such a full content, and with a sense
So apprehensive and discriminant,
As no temptation can intoxicate
Nor have I even terror at the thought
That I am clasped by such a saintliness.

ANGEL

All praise to Him, at whose sublime decree
    The last are first, the first become the last ;

By whom the suppliant prisoner is set free,
  By whom proud first-borns from their thrones are cast ;
  Who raises Mary to be Queen of Heaven,
  While Lucifer is left, condemned and unforgiven.

III

SOUL

I will address him. Mighty one, my Lord,
My Guardian Spirit, all hail !

ANGEL

                    All hail, my child !
My child and brother, hail ! what wouldest thou ?

SOUL

I would have nothing but to speak with thee
For speaking's sake. I wish to hold with thee
Conscious communion ; though I fain would know
A maze of things, were it but meet to ask,
And not a curiousness.

ANGEL

                    You cannot now
Cherish a wish which ought not to be wished.

THE DREAM OF GERONTIUS

SOUL

Then I will speak. I ever had believed
That on the moment when the struggling soul
Quitted its mortal case, forthwith it fell
Under the awful Presence of its God,
There to be judged and sent to its own place.
What lets me now from going to my Lord ?

ANGEL

Thou art not let ; but with extremest speed
Art hurrying to the Just and Holy Judge :
For scarcely art thou disembodied yet.
Divide a moment, as men measure time,
Into its million-million-millionth part,
Yet even less than that the interval
Since thou didst leave the body ; and the priest
Cried " Subvenite," and they fell to prayer ;
Nay, scarcely yet have they begun to pray.

For spirits and men by different standards mete
The less and greater in the flow of time.
By sun and moon, primeval ordinances—
By stars which rise and set harmoniously—
By the recurring seasons, and the swing,

THE DREAM OF GERONTIUS

This way and that, of the suspended rod
Precise and punctual, men divide the hours,
Equal, continuous, for their common use.
Not so with us in the immaterial world ;
But intervals in their succession
Are measured by the living thought alone,
And grow or wane with its intensity.
And time is not a common property ;
But what is long is short, and swift is slow,
And near is distant, as received and grasped
By this mind and by that, and every one
Is standard of his own chronology.
And memory lacks its natural resting-points
Of years, and centuries, and periods.
It is thy very energy of thought
Which keeps thee from thy God.

SOUL

                        Dear Angel, say,
Why have I now no fear at meeting Him ?
Along my earthly life, the thought of death
And judgment was to me most terrible.
I had it aye before me, and I saw
The Judge severe e'en in the crucifix.

Along my earthly life, the thought of death
And judgment was to me most terrible.
I had it aye before me, and I saw
The judge severe e'en in the Crucifix.

THE DREAM OF GERONTIUS

Now that the hour is come, my fear is fled ;
And at this balance of my destiny,
Now close upon me, I can forward look
With a serenest joy.

ANGEL

It is because
Then thou didst fear, that now thou dost not fear.
Thou hast forestalled the agony, and so
For thee the bitterness of death is past.
Also, because already in thy soul
The judgment is begun. That day of doom,
One and the same for the collected world—
That solemn consummation for all flesh,
Is, in the case of each, anticipate
Upon his death ; and, as the last great day
In the particular judgment is rehearsed,
So now too, ere thou comest to the Throne,
A presage falls upon thee, as a ray
Straight from the Judge, expressive of thy lot.
That calm and joy uprising in thy soul
Is first-fruit to thee of thy recompense,
And heaven begun.

IV

SOUL

But hark! upon my sense
Comes a fierce hubbub, which would make me fear,
Could I be frighted.

ANGEL

We are now arrived
Close on the judgment court; that sullen howl
Is from the demons who assemble there.
It is the middle region, where of old
Satan appeared among the sons of God,
To cast his jibes and scoffs at holy Job.
So now his legions throng the vestibule,
Hungry and wild, to claim their property,
And gather souls for hell. Hist to their cry.

SOUL

How sour and how uncouth a dissonance!

DEMONS

Low-born clods
Of brute earth,
They aspire
To become gods,

THE DREAM OF GERONTIUS

By a new birth,
And an extra grace,
And a score of merits.
As if aught
Could stand in place
Of the high thought,
And the glance of fire
Of the great spirits,
The powers blest,
The lords by right,
The primal owners,
Of the proud dwelling
And realm of light,—
Dispossessed,
Aside thrust,
Chucked down,
By the sheer might
Of a despot's will,
Of a tyrant's frown,
Who after expelling
Their hosts, gave,
Triumphant still,
And still unjust,
Each forfeit crown

THE DREAM OF GERONTIUS

To psalm-droners,
And canting groaners,
To every slave,
And pious cheat,
And crawling knave,
Who licked the dust
Under his feet.

ANGEL

It is the restless panting of their being ;
Like beasts of prey, who, caged within their bars,
In a deep hideous purring have their life,
And an incessant pacing to and fro.

DEMONS

The mind bold
And independent,
The purpose free,
So we are told,
Must not think
To have the ascendant.
What's a saint ?
One whose breath
Doth the air taint
Before his death ;

A bundle of bones,
Which fools adore,
Ha ! ha !
When life is o'er,
Which rattle and stink,
E'en in the flesh.
We cry his pardon !
No flesh hath he ;
Ha ! ha !
For it hath died,
'Tis crucified
Day by day,
Afresh, afresh,
Ha ! ha !
That holy clay,
Ha ! ha !
This gains guerdon,
So priestlings prate,
Ha ! ha !
Before the Judge,
And pleads and atones
For spite and grudge,
And bigot mood,
And envy and hate,
And greed of blood.

THE DREAM OF GERONTIUS

SOUL

How impotent they are ! and yet on earth
They have repute for wondrous power and skill ;
And books describe, how that the very face
Of the Evil One, if seen, would have a force
Even to freeze the blood, and choke the life
Of him who saw it.

ANGEL
                              In thy trial-state
Thou hadst a traitor nestling close at home,
Connatural, who with the powers of hell
Was leagued, and of thy senses kept the keys,
And to that deadliest foe unlocked thy heart.
And therefore is it, in respect of man,
Those fallen ones show so majestical.
But, when some child of grace, angel or saint,
Pure and upright in his integrity
Of nature, meets the demons on their raid,
They scud away as cowards from the fight.
Nay, oft hath holy hermit in his cell,
Not yet disburdened of mortality,
Mocked at their threats and warlike overtures ;
Or, dying, when they swarmed, like flies, around,
Defied them, and departed to his Judge.

THE DREAM OF GERONTIUS

    Virtue and vice,
     A knave's pretence,
      'Tis all the same ;
     Ha ! ha !
      Dread of hell-fire,
     Of the venomous flame,
      A coward's plea.
    Give him his price,
      Saint though he be,
     Ha ! ha !
     From shrewd good sense
      He'll slave for hire ;
     Ha ! ha !
      And does but aspire
    To the heaven above
      With sordid aim,
    And not from love.
     Ha ! ha !

SOUL

I see not those false spirits ; shall I see
My dearest Master, when I reach His throne ;
Or hear, at least, His awful judgment-word
With personal intonation, as I now

THE DREAM OF GERONTIUS

Hear thee, not see thee, Angel ? Hitherto
All has been darkness since I left the earth ;
Shall I remain thus sight bereft all through
My penance time ? If so, how comes it then
That I have hearing still, and taste, and touch,
Yet not a glimmer of that princely sense
Which binds ideas in one, and makes them live ?

ANGEL

Nor touch, nor taste, nor hearing hast thou now ;
Thou livest in a world of signs and types,
The presentations of most holy truths,
Living and strong, which now encompass thee.
A disembodied soul, thou hast by right
No converse with aught else beside thyself ;
But, lest so stern a solitude should load
And break thy being, in mercy are vouchsafed
Some lower measures of perception,
Which seem to thee, as though through channels brought,
Through ear, or nerves, or palate, which are gone.
And thou art wrapped and swathed around in dreams,
Dreams that are true, yet enigmatical ;
For the belongings of thy present state,
Save through such symbols, come not home to thee.

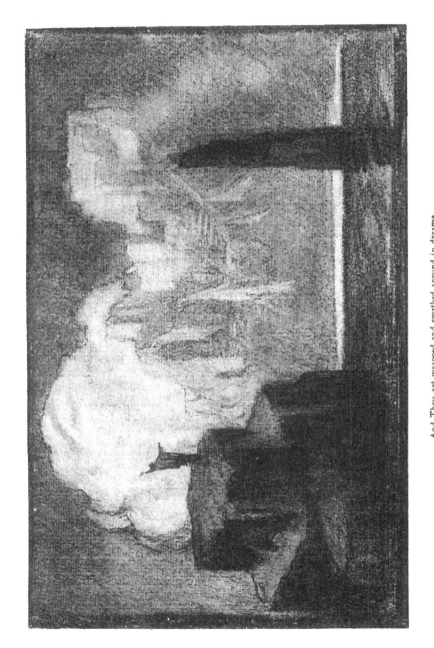

And Thou art wrapped and swathed around in dreams,
Dreams that are true, yet enigmatical.

And thus thou tell'st of space, and time, and size,
Of fragrant, solid, bitter, musical,
Of fire, and of refreshment after fire ;
As (let me use similitude of earth,
To aid thee in the knowledge thou dost ask)—
As ice which blisters may be said to burn.
Nor hast thou now extension, with its parts
Correlative,—long habit cozens thee,—
Nor power to move thyself, nor limbs to move.
Hast thou not heard of those, who, after loss
Of hand or foot, still cried that they had pains
In hand or foot, as though they had it still ?
So is it now with thee, who hast not lost
Thy hand or foot, but all which made up man ;
So will it be, until the joyous day
Of resurrection, when thou wilt regain
All thou hast lost, new-made and glorified.
How, even now, the consummated Saints
See God in heaven, I may not explicate.
Meanwhile let it suffice thee to possess
Such means of converse as are granted thee,
Though, till that Beatific Vision, thou art blind ;
For e'en thy purgatory, which comes like fire,
Is fire without its light.

THE DREAM OF GERONTIUS

SOUL
                    His will be done !
I am not worthy e'er to see again
The face of day ; far less His countenance
Who is the very sun. Nathless, in life,
When I looked forward to my purgatory,
It ever was my solace to believe
That, ere I plunged amid th' avenging flame,
I had one sight of Him to strengthen me.

ANGEL

Nor rash nor vain is that presentiment ;
Yes,—for one moment thou shalt see thy Lord.
Thus will it be : what time thou art arraigned
Before the dread tribunal, and thy lot
Is cast for ever, should it be to sit
On His right hand among His pure elect,
Then sight, or that which to the soul is sight,
As by a lightning-flash, will come to thee,
And thou shalt see, amid the dark profound,
Whom thy soul loveth, and would fain approach,—
One moment ; but thou knowest not, my child,
What thou dost ask : that sight of the Most Fair
Will gladden thee, but it will pierce thee too.

.... then sight or that to which thy soul is sight,
As by a lightning flash will come to thee ....

THE DREAM OF GERONTIUS

SOUL

Thou speakest darkly, Angel! and an awe
Falls on me, and a fear lest I be rash.

ANGEL

There was a mortal, who is now above
In the mid glory: he, when near to die,
Was given communion with the Crucified,—
Such, that the Master's very wounds were stamped
Upon his flesh; and, from the agony
Which thrilled through body and soul in that embrace
Learn that the flame of the Everlasting Love
Doth burn ere it transform. . . .

V

. . . Hark to those sounds!
They come of tender beings angelical,
Least and most childlike of the sons of God.

FIRST CHOIR OF ANGELICALS

Praise to the Holiest in the height,
And in the depth be praise:
In all His words most wonderful;
Most sure in all His ways!

THE DREAM OF GERONTIUS

To us His elder race He gave
   To battle and to win,
Without the chastisement of pain,
   Without the soil of sin.

The younger son He willed to be
   A marvel in his birth:
Spirit and flesh his parents were ;
   His home was heaven and earth.

The Eternal blessed His child, and armed,
   And sent him hence afar,
To serve as champion in the field
   Of elemental war,

To be His Viceroy in the world
   Of matter, and of sense ;
Upon the frontier, towards the foe,
   A resolute defence.

ANGEL

We now have passed the gate, and are within
The House of Judgment ; and whereas on earth
Temples and palaces are formed of parts
Costly and rare, but all material,

THE DREAM OF GERONTIUS

So in the world of spirits nought is found,
To mould withal and form into a whole,
But what is immaterial ; and thus
The smallest portions of this edifice,
Cornice, or frieze, or balustrade, or stair,
The very pavement is made up of life—
Of holy, blessed, and immortal beings,
Who hymn their Maker's praise continually.

SECOND CHOIR OF ANGELICALS

    Praise to the Holiest in the height,
      And in the depth be praise :
    In all His words most wonderful ;
      Most sure in all His ways !

    Woe to thee, man ! for he was found
      A recreant in the fight ;
    And lost his heritage of heaven,
      And fellowship with light.

    Above him now the angry sky,
      Around, the tempest's din ;
    Who once had angels for his friends,
      Had but the brutes for kin.

THE DREAM OF GERONTIUS

O man ! a savage kindred they ;
  To flee that monster brood
He scaled the seaside cave, and clomb
  The giants of the wood.

With now a fear, and now a hope,
  With aids which chance supplied,
From youth to eld, from sire to son,
  He lived, and toiled, and died.

He dreed his penance age by age ;
  And step by step began
Slowly to doff his savage garb,
  And be again a man.

And quickened by the Almighty's breath
  And chastened by His rod,
And taught by Angel-visitings,
  At length he sought his God ;

And learned to call upon His name,
  And in His faith create
A household and a fatherland,
  A city and a state.

And learned to call upon His name, . . .

THE DREAM OF GERONTIUS

Glory to Him who from the mire,
  In patient length of days,
Elaborated into life
  A people to His praise !

SOUL

The sound is like the rushing of the wind—
The summer wind among the lofty pines ;
Swelling and dying, echoing round about,
Now here, now distant, wild and beautiful ;
While, scattered from the branches it has stirred,
Descend ecstatic odours.

THIRD CHOIR OF ANGELICALS

Praise to the Holiest in the height,
  And in the depth be praise :
In all His words most wonderful ;
  Most sure in all His ways !

The Angels, as beseemingly
  To spirit-kind was given,
At once were tried and perfected,
  And took their seats in heaven.

THE DREAM OF GERONTIUS

For them no twilight or eclipse ;
   No growth and no decay ;
'Twas hopeless, all-ingulfing night,
   Or beatific day.

But to the younger race there rose
   A hope upon its fall ;
And slowly, surely, gracefully,
   The morning dawned on all.

And ages, opening out, divide
   The precious and the base,
And from the hard and sullen mass,
   Mature the heirs of grace.

O man ! albeit the quickening ray,
   Lit from his second birth,
Makes him at length what once he was,
   And heaven grows out of earth ;

Yet still between that earth and heaven—
   His journey and his goal—
A double agony awaits
   His body and his soul.

THE DREAM OF GERONTIUS

A double debt he has to pay—
  The forfeit of his sins,
The chill of death is past, and now
  The penance-fire begins.

Glory to Him, who evermore
  By truth and justice reigns ;
Who tears the soul from out its case,
  And burns away its stains !

ANGEL

They sing of thy approaching agony,
Which thou so eagerly didst question of :
It is the face of the Incarnate God
Shall smite thee with that keen and subtle pain ;
And yet the memory which it leaves will be
A sovereign febrifuge to heal the wound ;
And yet withal it will the wound provoke,
And aggravate and widen it the more.

SOUL

Thou speakest mysteries ; still methinks I know
To disengage the tangle of thy words :
Yet rather would I hear thy angel voice,
Than for myself be thy interpreter.

THE DREAM OF GERONTIUS

ANGEL

When then—if such thy lot—thou seest thy Judge,
The sight of Him will kindle in thy heart,
All tender, gracious, reverential thoughts.
Thou wilt be sick with love, and yearn for Him,
And feel as though thou couldst but pity Him,
That one so sweet should e'er have placed Himself
At disadvantage such, as to be used
So vilely by a being so vile as thee.
There is a pleading in His pensive eyes
Will pierce thee to the quick, and trouble thee.
And thou wilt hate and loathe thyself; for, though
Now sinless, thou wilt feel that thou hast sinned,
As never thou didst feel; and will desire
To slink away, and hide thee from His sight,
And yet wilt have a longing aye to dwell
Within the beauty of His countenance.
And these two pains, so counter and so keen,—
The longing for Him, when thou seest Him not;
The shame of self at thought of seeing Him,—
Will be thy veriest, sharpest purgatory.

SOUL

My soul is in my hand: I have no fear,—
In His dear might prepared for weal or woe.

But hark ! a grand mysterious harmony :
It floods me, like the deep and solemn sound
Of many waters.

ANGEL

    We have gained the stairs
Which rise towards the Presence-chamber ; there
A band of mighty Angels keep the way
On either side, and hymn the Incarnate God.

ANGELS OF THE SACRED STAIR

Father, whose goodness none can know, but they
 Who see Thee face to face,
By man hath come the infinite display
 Of Thy victorious grace ;
But fallen man—the creature of a day—
 Skills not that love to trace.
It needs, to tell the triumph Thou hast wrought,
An Angel's deathless fire, an Angel's reach of thought.

It needs that very Angel, who with awe,
 Amid the garden shade,
The great Creator in His sickness saw,
 Soothed by a creature's aid,
And agonised, as victim of the Law
 Which He Himself had made ;

For who can praise Him in His depth and height,
But he who saw Him reel amid that solitary fight ?

SOUL

Hark ! for the lintels of the Presence-gate
Are vibrating and echoing back the strain.

FOURTH CHOIR OF ANGELICALS

Praise to the Holiest in the height,
  And in the depth be praise :
In all His words most wonderful ;
  Most sure in all His ways !

The foe blasphemed the Holy Lord,
  As if He reckoned ill,
In that He placed His puppet man
  The frontier place to fill.

For even in his best estate,
  With amplest gifts endued,
A sorry sentinel was he,
  A being of flesh and blood.

As though a thing, who for his help
  Must needs possess a wife,
Could cope with those proud rebel hosts,
  Who had angelic life.

We have gained the stairs
Which rise towards the Presence Chamber; there
A band of mighty Angels keep the way
On either side, and hymn the Incarnate God.

And when, by blandishment of Eve,
   That earth-born Adam fell,
He shrieked in triumph, and he cried,
   " A sorry sentinel;

The Maker by His word is bound,
   Escape or cure is none;
He must abandon to his doom,
   And slay His darling Son."

ANGEL

And now the threshold, as we traverse it,
Utters aloud its glad responsive chant.

FIFTH CHOIR OF ANGELICALS

   Praise to the Holiest in the height,
      And in the depth be praise:
   In all His words most wonderful;
      Most sure in all His ways!

   O loving wisdom of our God!
      When all was sin and shame,
   A second Adam to the fight
      And to the rescue came.

THE DREAM OF GERONTIUS

O wisest love ! that flesh and blood
   Which did in Adam fail,
Should strive afresh against the foe,
   Should strive and should prevail ;

And that a higher gift than grace
   Should flesh and blood refine,
God's Presence and His very Self,
   And Essence all divine.

O generous love ! that He who smote
   In man for man the foe,
The double agony in man
   For man should undergo ;

And in the garden secretly,
   And on the cross on high,
Should teach His brethren and inspire
   To suffer and to die.

VI

ANGEL

Thy judgment now is near, for we are come
Into the veiled presence of our God.

SOUL

I hear the voices that I left on earth.

ANGEL

It is the voice of friends around thy bed,
Who say the " Subvenite " with the priest.
Hither the echoes come ; before the Throne
Stands the great Angel of the Agony,
The same who strengthened Him, what time He knelt
Lone in the garden shade, bedewed with blood.
The Angel best can plead with Him for all
Tormented souls, the dying and the dead.

ANGEL OF THE AGONY

Jesu ! by that shuddering dread which fell on Thee ;
Jesu ! by that cold dismay which sickened Thee ;
Jesu ! by that pang of heart which thrilled in Thee ;

Jesu ! by that mount of sins which crippled Thee ;
Jesu ! by that sense of guilt which stifled Thee ;
Jesu ! by that innocence which girdled Thee ;
Jesu ! by that sanctity which reigned in Thee ;
Jesu ! by that Godhead which was one with Thee ;
Jesu ! spare these souls which are so dear to Thee,
Who in prison, calm and patient, wait for Thee ;
Hasten, Lord, their hour, and bid them come to Thee,
To that glorious Home, where they shall ever gaze on Thee.

SOUL

I go before my Judge. Ah ! . . .

ANGEL
    . . . Praise to His Name !
The eager spirit has darted from my hold,
And, with the intemperate energy of love,
Flies to the dear feet of Emmanuel ;
But, ere it reach them, the keen sanctity,
Which with its effluence, like a glory, clothes
And circles round the Crucified, has seized,
And scorched, and shrivelled it ; and now it lies
Passive and still before the awful Throne.
O happy, suffering soul ! for it is safe,
Consumed, yet quickened, by the glance of God.

SOUL

Take me away, and in the lowest deep
    There let me be,
And there in hope the lone night-watches keep,
    Told out for me.
There, motionless and happy in my pain,
    Lone, not forlorn,—
There will I sing my sad perpetual strain,
    Until the morn.
There will I sing, and soothe my stricken breast,
    Which ne'er can cease
To throb, and pine, and languish, till possest
    Of its Sole Peace.
There will I sing my absent Lord and Love :—
    Take me away,
That sooner I may rise, and go above,
And see Him in the truth of everlasting day.

VII

ANGEL

Now let the golden prison ope its gates,
Making sweet music, as each fold revolves
Upon its ready hinge. And ye great powers,

THE DREAM OF GERONTIUS

Angels of Purgatory, receive from me
My charge, a precious soul, until the day,
When, from all bond and forfeiture released,
I shall reclaim it for the courts of light.

SOULS IN PURGATORY

1. Lord, Thou hast been our refuge; in every generation;

2. Before the hills were born, and the world was: from age to age Thou art God.

3. Bring us not, Lord, very low: for Thou hast said, Come back again, ye sons of Adam.

4. A thousand years before Thine eyes are but as yesterday: and as a watch of the night which is come and gone.

5. The grass springs up in the morning: at evening-tide it shrivels up and dies.

6. So we fail in Thine anger: and in Thy wrath we are troubled.

7. Thou hast set our sins in Thy sight: and our round of days in the light of Thy countenance.

Take me away, and in the lowest deep
There let me be.

8. Come back, O Lord! how long: and be entreated for Thy servants.

9. In Thy morning we shall be filled with Thy mercy: we shall rejoice and be in pleasure all our days.

10. We shall be glad according to the days of our humiliation: and the years in which we have seen evil.

11. Look, O Lord, upon Thy servants and on Thy work: and direct their children.

12. And let the beauty of the Lord our God be upon us: and the work of our hands, establish Thou it.

Glory be to the Father, and to the Son, and to the Holy Ghost.

As it was in the beginning, is now, and ever shall be: world without end. Amen.

ANGEL

Softly and gently, dearly-ransomed soul,
 In my most loving arms I now enfold thee,
And, o'er the penal waters, as they roll,
 I poise thee, and I lower thee, and hold thee.

93

THE DREAM OF GERONTIUS

And carefully I dip thee in the lake,
   And thou, without a sob or a resistance,
Dost through the flood thy rapid passage take,
   Sinking deep, deeper, into the dim distance.

Angels, to whom the willing task is given,
   Shall tend, and nurse, and lull thee, as thou liest ;
And Masses on the earth, and prayers in heaven,
   Shall aid thee at the Throne of the Most Highest.

Farewell, but not for ever ! brother dear,
   Be brave and patient on thy bed of sorrow ;
Swiftly shall pass thy night of trial here,
   And I will come and wake thee on the morrow.

Lightning Source UK Ltd.
Milton Keynes UK
UKOW06n0444231115

263326UK00012B/173/P